TO

FROM

THE

Husband Book

THE

Husband Book

A Guy's Guide to Marriage

HARRY HARRISON, JR.

**Andrews McMeel
Publishing**

Kansas City

The Husband Book:

A Guy's Guide to Marriage

02 03 04 05 06 BIN 10 9 8 7 6 5 4 3 2 1

Book design by Holly Camerlinck

Library of Congress Cataloging-in-Publication Data

Harrison, Harry H.
    The husband book : a guy's guide to marriage / Harry Harrison, Jr.
       p. cm.
    ISBN 0-7407-2235-2
 1. Marriage. 2. Husbands—Conduct of life. I. Title.
    HQ734 .H327 2002
    646.7'8—dc21   2002019799

CONTENTS

Contents

Contents

Contents

THE

Husband Book

INTRODUCTION

*A*s every husband knows, a wife is the most puzzling, baffling, engaging, mysterious, complex, wonderful creation God put on this earth. It's an established fact that men who are married tend to live longer . . . though they lose more sleep, spend more money, and work longer hours than their single brothers.

A wife can make you feel like the most special person on earth and then minutes later have you groping in the medicine cabinet for pain killers. A wife can be your best friend, your lover, your true companion, your biggest fan, or she can be a creature rising from the depths of PMS to scorch the earth like no nuclear bomb ever could.

That's the trick to being a husband. It starts with finding a woman to marry you. She'll tell you she loves you. Then she'll leave it up to you to figure out everything else.

Start Here

Don't talk about your old girlfriends.

It would be best not to invite them to the wedding either.

Don't assume when you are married things will stay the same as when you were dating. Things change from the moment you say,

"I do."

Agree from the beginning to never lie to each other.

Remember these words:

"*Your hair looks great.*"

$\mathcal{D}$on't expect lifelong bliss, free from problems, quarrels, or issues. You're guaranteed to be disappointed.

$\mathcal{R}$ealize from the beginning love is a decision.

$\mathcal{D}$on't be surprised when the woman who wants satin lingerie in her twenties wants cotton flannel p.j.'s in her forties.

● ● ●

$\mathcal{R}$emember no matter how much you love her, a wife cannot be your complete source of happiness or sorrow. Or else you will have nothing but sorrow.

Start Here

Keep in mind the two greatest obstacles to your happiness will be romance and finance.

◆ ◆ ◆

Don't think that just because you're married you have to do *everything* together. In fact, it's important that you don't do everything together.

*R*emember you're going to spend the next fifty or so years in conversation with her, interrupted by life.

♦ ♦ ♦

*D*on't make the mistake of picking out your first apartment without her. In fact, don't make the mistake of making any major decisions without her.

Start Here

$\mathcal{D}$on't ever come between her

and her *hairdresser.*

Unless she comes home
after spending two hundred dollars
and looks no different.

Start praying from your first night
of marriage together. As a couple.

● ● ●

Show her respect at all times.
Even when you're furious with her.

Start Here

Shower often.

◆ ◆ ◆

Let her find a scented candle burning
when she gets up in the morning.
It sets the tone for the day.

*F*or some reason, she'll think
the pair of shoes that are the most

uncomfortable

look the best on her.

Help her work through this.

Start Here

Don't fantasize about other women.

This falls into the *"stupid"* category.

Don't compare her to other women,

mentally, verbally, now, or ever.

This falls into the

" I'm looking for a fight "

category.

She will want you to read her mind.
You will fail more often than not.
Just accept this and move on.

She will want to talk about feelings. You will
want to talk about football. Here's a perfect
chance to learn the art of compromise.

Start Here

*T*ell her you *love* her
more than you think you need to.
Like four or five times day.

Incredibly, she will hear you
maybe once a day, but that will be enough.

$\mathcal{T}$ake her shopping often and buy her outfits she would never buy herself.

● ● ●

$\mathcal{D}$on't fall into the trap of thinking you'll be happy if only she'll be happy.

Start Here

*I*f and when she has a fight with her mother, do not take sides. In fact, go outside.

♦ ♦ ♦

*S*end her flowers. With a truly sappy card. For some reason, women love this.

$\mathcal{T}$alk about your plans and dreams with her.

Listen to hers.

♦ ♦ ♦

$\mathcal{F}$lirt with her continually.

Remember, that's how all this got started.

Start Here

*R*ealize you're not marrying a cook or a maid or a fantasy, but a woman with her own dreams and fears and expectations.

*S*tart saving money.

*I*f you don't know what to buy her,
buy her jewelry.

*W*ork on yourself.

Start Here

$\mathcal{T}$ry as you might, you won't be able to buy her happiness. So have a plan B.

• • •

$\mathcal{W}$ait to have children. They deserve to have stable parents who've worked the kinks out.

*W*hile you're young, travel all you can. Because when you're older, there'll be kids, obligations, and let's face it, a lingering desire to catch up on your sleep.

● ● ●

*D*on't criticize her in front of others. This can have far-reaching consequences.

Start Here

$\mathcal{D}$on't try to change her.

$\mathcal{B}$efore you buy her chocolate,
find out if she's allergic to it.

*I*f a couple can successfully share one
bathroom, one sink, one tub, and one shower,
the odds are good they'll stay married.

♦ ♦ ♦

*D*on't let her parents or
your parents buy you too much.
Gifts usually come with strings.

Start Here

*G*et to know her mom.

Send her *flowers* every now and then.

(Huge number of brownie points.)

*R*emember she married you to be with you.
Not to get cell-phone calls from the duck blind.

● ● ●

*B*uy her a diamond. Even if you have to
wait twenty years to do so.

$\mathcal{L}$et her buy you cologne.

♦ ♦ ♦

$\mathcal{R}$emember a lot of men are incapable
of filling out forms. Let her.

*I*f you have to introduce her to the world
of sports, explain the rules. Many women
find football as difficult to understand
as men do *La Bohème.*

♦ ♦ ♦

*B*e able to live without her. This way you
can love her without owning her.

Start Here

*D*on't forget she will never understand your fascination for bodily noises. Never.

*R*emember you don't own her. She's your wife, not your possession. She's entitled to her own opinions, her own beliefs, even her own mistakes.

*D*on't make fun of her.

• • •

*A*ccept the fact that she may not like
all your friends. In fact, if she likes only one
or two, count yourself lucky.

Start Here

$\mathcal{D}$on't walk in front of her.

◆ ◆ ◆

$\mathcal{H}$elp her chase her dreams.
This could be going back to college,
starting a company, or writing a book.

$\mathcal{A}$s often as you can,
make her feel adored.

$\mathcal{R}$emember many women are not
huge fans of Sylvester Stallone movies.
Strange, but true.

Start Here

$\mathcal{D}$evelop a sense of humor. Happily married
couples laugh most of the time.

• • •

$\mathcal{D}$ecide who will be in charge of the family
finances. And before you decide that it should
be you, figure out who has the most discipline,
self-control, and math skills. (Is this really you?)

*L*earn to compromise on the temperature inside your home.

*I*f your wife is in charge of the finances, respect her opinion about what is affordable.

Start Here

$\mathcal{I}$f you're in charge of the money,
respect the fact that your wife is entitled to shop,
to buy, and to enjoy life without
an editorial from you.

♦ ♦ ♦

$\mathcal{D}$on't try to control her moods.

*R*emember your actions say as much

about your *feelings* for her

as your words do.

But women still like to hear the words.

*D*o not make her your god, nor should you become hers. You are her husband, and to become anything more or less than that will change your marriage for the worse.

*Y*our looking like Arnold Schwarzenegger will be much more important to you than to her.

*D*on't try to control what she thinks, says, or even does. It's akin to trying to control a forest fire.

*E*ncourage her to have her own group of friends. You can't imagine how important they will be to her.

Start Here

$\mathcal{B}$uy an electric blanket
with dual controls.

• • •

$\mathcal{D}$on't keep score.

*R*emember the strongest marriages are made up of two independent people who love each other, not two needy people who are dependent upon each other.

*U*se deodorant.

Start Here

41

Remember, she will always be able to
sense when you're disturbed. If you've had
a lousy day or something went wrong,
tell her, or else she'll think you're mad at her.

Don't belittle her ever,
not in front of her friends,
not among your friends.

*R*ealize a woman's intrinsic *nature* is to guard her nest. Anything that threatens that nest will quickly turn her from a peaceful sparrow to an enraged, furious, AK-47-packing kamikaze pilot.

The best tip here is to get out of her way.

Start Here

*I*f she tends to get seasick,
your buying a boat will only result in her
throwing up in your new boat.

♦ ♦ ♦

*R*emember that contrary to what most men
believe, you will not spontaneously erupt into
having a period when you have to go to the store
alone to buy tampons.

*D*on't marry her thinking
you can change her.

♦ ♦ ♦

*D*on't go to bed mad. This can
cause fights to last as long as a week.
And bad memories to last years.

Start Here

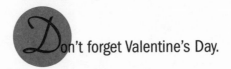

Don't forget Valentine's Day.

Always let her know
how important she is to you,
how much you treasure her.

$\mathcal{L}$et her paint the house the color she likes.
Even if it's yellow.

● ● ●

$\mathcal{G}$ive her the nice car.
And wash it for her now and then.

Start Here

Don't take everything she says in anger personally. In fact, it's best to practice being deaf during these times.

♦ ♦ ♦

Celebrate her successes, even the smallest ones, and you'll be astonished at how successful she becomes.

*E*very now and then,
give her the remote control.

(If this results in *hyperventilation*,
try deep breathing.)

Start Here

*T*alk to her about her dreams
as well as yours.

*W*atch her dumb romantic movies,
especially if she watches your
dumb violent ones.

*R*emember, just because she goes to
football games and baseball games and
basketball games doesn't necessarily mean
she likes them. She may just like being with you.

• • •

*D*on't ever think you know more
than she does.

Start Here

$\mathcal{T}$ake her to the ballet.

♦ ♦ ♦

$\mathcal{T}$ake walks with her . . . even if you
hate walks. This is a wonderful time
to hear what's on her mind.

*D*on't get involved in any fights between her and her parents. Just listen to her.

*B*uy her perfume.

Start Here

*V*ideotape her from day one.

*R*ealize how busy she is and offer to help.

*R*efrain from doing or saying anything
that would hurt her self-esteem.

● ● ●

*B*uy the clothes she says you look good in.
If you're not dressing for her,
who are you dressing for?

Start Here

*I*f you don't know where to take her,
take her to Hawaii.

*D*o the laundry sometimes.
Just because she usually does it
doesn't mean she likes doing it.

*B*uy her a cell phone.

*T*reasure your free time with her . . .
like when the two of you are just
lying in bed waking up.

Start Here

57

Write her love letters.
Even after twenty-five years.

♦ ♦ ♦

Remember a man's greatest failing is
usually his failure to listen.

Strive for personal happiness . . .
even when she's not.

♦ ♦ ♦

Encourage her to reach for the stars.

Start Here

*H*ug her. All the time.
Especially when you don't
feel like hugging her.

● ● ●

*D*on't try to give her everything.
This will only make you tired, bitter, and broke.

*M*ake her aware that she's a big part of your success. Because whether you admit it or not, she is.

● ● ●

*N*ever let the romance dim and the love won't either.

Start Here

Romance her with a walk in the park.

Don't wear headphones.

*S*mile. Say "thank you." Enjoy every moment.

*Y*ou will notice that women think all men
have ESP and they'll get upset with you
when your powers have deserted you.
This is the reason to keep talking to her.

Start Here

Remember these words:

"*I think you look great in that.*"

Spirituality

$\mathcal{D}$evelop a spiritual program.
There will be times when it carries
your marriage.

♦ ♦ ♦

$\mathcal{M}$ake a tithe commitment to God,
whether it's to a church, a charity,
or something else.

*P*ray nightly with her.

● ● ●

*P*ray daily for her.

● ● ●

*B*e able to turn her life and her wants
and her fears over to God.

*A*sk her for help.

• • •

*R*ealize she has her own beliefs. Let her be.

• • •

*B*e honest.

Spirituality

*R*ead a devotional every day. Together.

◆ ◆ ◆

*R*emember a loving marriage is
something alive. You have to nourish it daily.

◆ ◆ ◆

*W*hatever you look for in her, you'll find.

$\mathcal{A}$ccept the fact you can't please her all
the time, you can't make her happy all the time,
you can't have the right answers all the time.
You can just love her for all time.

$\mathcal{T}$alk to her about God,
about your faith, about what you believe.
She needs to hear this.

Sit outside with her and watch a sunset.

• • •

Go on a spiritual retreat.
Make conscious contact with God.

• • •

Talk to her about the events and people that
have shaped your life.

*K*eep no secrets.

● ● ●

*C*all her every night you're away from home.
Even if you're on the other side of the world.

● ● ●

*R*emind her of her successes, her intelligence,
her accomplishments.

Spirituality

Every morning thank God for the

myriad of ways she's changed your life.

(For instance, most men would be
wearing double-knit suits if it weren't for
the women in their lives.)

*W*hen she comes home tired, hungry, and angry, you may be the nearest available target. Handle with care.

♦ ♦ ♦

*E*ncourage her to further her own spirituality.

♦ ♦ ♦

*C*herish her everyday. Consciously.

Spirituality

*P*ick a church or temple or synagogue
that the two of you can attend regularly,
support financially, and grow with spiritually.

*T*each a youth group together. You'll learn
about kids before you have them.

Arguments

*R*emember love is work.

● ● ●

*B*ut love is also kind.

● ● ●

*D*on't expect your marriage to be
conflict free.

Arguments

*B*efore the fight escalates into World War Three,
ask yourself: How important is it?

♦ ♦ ♦

*P*ractice patience with her moods,
her fears, her worries. They're not going anywhere.

$\mathcal{D}$on't bring up *ancient* history.

It's never once ended a fight.

*M*ake sure she hears exactly
what you're saying. Have her repeat your words.
It will amaze you what she's heard.

*W*hen she's truly furious,
realize you can't win. Surrender.

Don't pout. Not manly.

Generally speaking, if you agree with her,
fights can be averted.

Arguments

*F*orgive her. Even if it's the last thing you want to do. Especially when you don't think she deserves it.

*A*ccept the fact women argue differently than men. She'll threaten to leave. She'll say truly insane things. It's her right as a woman.

*R*emember that if you think

it just might be your fault, it probably is.

● ● ●

*S*creaming back won't help.

Arguments

*I*f you ever feel like pushing or hitting her,
seek immediate counseling.

*R*ealize that there will be days
when her hormones will be in control of her mind.
Love her anyway.

Remember if you don't say anything mean,
that's one less thing you'll have to apologize for.

When *conflicts* do arise,
ask yourself, "Would you rather
be right or happy?"

People who would rather be right
end up in divorce court.

*L*earn to ask for forgiveness and mean it. She may make you say it all day and night, but eventually she will forgive.

♦ ♦ ♦

*R*emember while men just want to solve the problem, women want to talk about how it makes them feel. While this may set your teeth on edge, your job is to sit and listen.

Arguments

*P*ray together at night, even when you're mad.
This keeps priorities straight.

● ● ●

*D*on't bring up the past. In fact,
a short memory is a good thing here.

*L*earn to accept her *apologies*.

Even if you think she could have
done better.

$\mathcal{D}$on't take to heart anything
she says during an argument.

♦ ♦ ♦

$\mathcal{P}$ractice saying the words "I'm sorry"
and "I forgive you." These phrases tend
to paralyze the lips of most men.

*L*earn you don't have to win.

♦ ♦ ♦

*D*on't use words to harm.

♦ ♦ ♦

*J*ust because she's hostile doesn't mean
you have to be.

Arguments

*D*on't try to control her friends,
her moods, her spending, her happiness.

*C*oncentrate on your issues
and you'll both be happier.

*P*ractice kindness, patience, and gentleness all the time.

*R*ealize she has an emotional need for affection—not to be confused with hopping into bed—and if you meet this, a lot of fights can be avoided.

Arguments

*R*emember these words:

"*You could be right.*"

Pregnancy and Childbirth

*M*eet her doctors. Let them know
there's a husband who cares.

*N*ever, ever tell her she could
lose a few pounds.

*R*emember, having a baby is nothing like it is on TV. It can take days.

● ● ●

*B*e prepared for a dry run or two to the hospital.

*S*he will crave some very strange food
at two A.M.: cottage cheese with
French dressing and hot peppers
and ginger snaps.

Hold your *breath* and make it for her.

You will want to spend *weekends* watching the game. She will want to spend them in baby-supply stores.

You lose.

*T*ell yourself putting a crib together
is training for putting a Big Wheel together.

♦ ♦ ♦

*E*ncourage her to exercise,
to continue to take care of herself.

*C*ommit yourself to giving her a back rub
every night during pregnancy until
your arms feel like they're going to fall off.
This is where you can share her pain.

*T*his is not a time to be bringing home
Sports Illustrated's swimsuit issue.

$\mathcal{T}$ell her how beautiful she is during pregnancy, even when she's big, grumpy, and sporting a truly odd hairdo.

$\mathcal{R}$emember the two of you will spend her nine months of pregnancy on completely different planes.

*A*sk yourself how you would like to carry a baby around for nine months, throwing up, swelling, unable to sit up or lie down and being regularly patted by strangers and prodded by doctors. She feels the same way.

$\mathcal{G}$o to birthing classes with her. Pay attention.
Help her practice her breathing.

● ● ●

$\mathcal{D}$on't panic when there's all this chaos
in the delivery room. Remember, the doctors
have done this before.

$\mathcal{T}$he labor room will scare both of you.

And that *screaming* is from the
woman down the hall having
natural childbirth.

$\mathcal{D}$on't faint. Bad start.

♦ ♦ ♦

$\mathcal{F}$ill her room with flowers. Overspend.
She'll never forget it.

♦ ♦ ♦

$\mathcal{Y}$ou'll be incredulous at your wife's capacity
for loving this child. It will blow you away.

Pregnancy and Childbirth

*B*uy Dr. Spock's book. He has all the answers right now. You have none.

• • •

*I*f it's a boy, don't assume your name will be his. She may love you a lot more than your name.

• • •

*D*on't worry. Her body will bounce back.

Children

Kids cost a fortune. Know that going in.

♦ ♦ ♦

If she wants to quit work after the baby
is born, don't discourage her. Move into
a smaller home, reduce your expenses,
and let her be a full-time mom.

Be ready to spring out of bed at all hours of the night—for a very long time.

Limit your business travel immediately after the baby is born.

*L*earn to do all of the following
in the dark: navigate bedrooms,
bathrooms, stairways, and hallways;
warm a bottle; and calm down
a *screaming* baby.

Hey, she knows how.

Children

*A*ccept diaper duty. Without complaining.
It doesn't smell any better to her.

*R*esolve to be a part of this family,
the protector of these people,
to not go AWOL on them.

*I*f she seems extraordinarily depressed right after the baby is born, call her doctor. It's not you. It's not the baby. It's chemical.

• • •

*D*on't burp the baby in any shirt you want to wear that week.

Children

*R*ealize how utterly exhausting
caring for a newborn can be, especially for
a mother just out of the hospital.

♦ ♦ ♦

*M*ake sure she gets sleep.

♦ ♦ ♦

*M*ake sure your children grow up treating
both of you with respect.

*O*ffer to drive the car pool.

♦ ♦ ♦

*B*e understanding at the end of the day
if she has a lot to talk about. You may be
the first adult she's seen in ten hours.

♦ ♦ ♦

*B*uy a Volvo.

Children

*R*emember, children need clothes
and shoes and food and toys and all kinds
of stuff you never had to buy before
you had kids.

Don't *complain*.

Don't expect any help from her in teaching your kids to face adversity. A mother's instinct is to protect them from adversity.

Take the kids out for doughnuts on Saturdays so she can sleep.

Children

*B*e aware that kids treat their moms and dads differently. That's due to the fact that dads and moms treat their kids differently.

And that's good.

$\mathcal{D}$rive the kids to practice.
And don't complain about it.

● ● ●

$\mathcal{D}$on't let your kids play one parent
against the other. Ever.

$\mathcal{D}$ecide together on how you're going
to raise your children: bedtime, nutrition,
discipline, and so on. Then don't let
a two-year-old talk you out of it.

♦ ♦ ♦

$\mathcal{A}$lways be aware of how much
she does for the family.

*W*hen you move (and with a child you will move) walk around the new neighborhood. It's a great way to meet the neighbors and be with the family.

Children

*D*on't argue in front of the kids.

*D*on't make her the homework queen.
Everyone can use your help.

Hug her frequently
in front of the kids.

This makes everybody in the house
feel good (though the kids may say
they're grossed out).

*D*on't ever demean her
in front of the children. Ever.

● ● ●

*S*he may have secrets with the kids.
It just means they trust her.

*M*ake sure they give their mother gifts
and cards on Mother's Day and Christmas
and her birthday.

*R*ealize that even the kindest, gentlest,
most loving moms tend to get testy if they
don't take vacations regularly.

Children

*D*on't miss the PTA meetings, the "Meet the Teacher" nights, or school conferences.

*R*emember, your sons are watching how you treat a wife, and your daughters are watching how a wife is to be treated.

$\mathcal{T}$urn the TV off and talk with your family.
These are moments that can't be recaptured.

♦ ♦ ♦

$\mathcal{D}$on't expect her to share your
enthusiasm for coaching.

♦ ♦ ♦

$\mathcal{T}$each the kids to drive.

Children

*B*e prepared that as each child leaves home,
she may fall apart.

● ● ●

*O*n the other hand, she may have
to put you back together.

In-Laws

*S*he will think your parents are *goofy;*

you will think hers are *lock-up* material.

You will both be right.

*N*ever, ever say she's like her mom.

♦ ♦ ♦

*D*on't be stunned if her father looks
and acts a little like you.

♦ ♦ ♦

*S*ince you love her, chances are good
you'll love her brothers and sisters.

*N*ever forget she's big on family stuff.
Thanksgiving, Christmas, birthdays, vacations.
She wants to be surrounded by those
who love her.

♦ ♦ ♦

*I*f she's just had a rip-roaring scream-out
with her mom, you have two options:
seek shelter or comfort her.
Neither decision will really be right.

In-Laws

She will take seriously every niece's, cousin's, aunt's, and uncle's birthday and Christmas gift. Don't gripe about the costs.

If talking to her mom really unnerves her, that's reason enough for caller ID.

*H*er mother will give you
some truly *strange* gifts.
Smile and nod.

*I*f she wants to give her parents money,
be gentle here. She knows your
bank account balance.

*R*emember in-laws can be
a huge advantage—baby-sitters.

Problems

*I*f you focus on her defects,
they will only grow in your mind.

*E*ven if she's wrong,
let go of the compulsion to control her.

Problems

Focus on what's *good* and
right and *wonderful* about her.

Soon that's all you'll be able to see.

*Y*our happiness shouldn't rest on what she thinks of you. You can avoid a huge fight by not forcing her to see your sainthood.

*L*ow self-esteem can lead to fighting. If you feel bad about yourself, you'll feel bad about her.

Problems

*I*f every time you drink you have
a fight with her, stop drinking.

• • •

*I*f your marriage was founded on drinking,
sex, and parties, don't be stunned when things
go south in a couple of years.

$\mathcal{N}$ever go through her *purse*.
It's none of your business what's in there.

You won't be able to figure it out anyway.

*N*ever read her diary or her letters
unless she gives them to you.
You don't want to know.

*S*he'll tolerate your being sick
for a couple of days. After that,
get up and go to work.

*Y*ou're entitled to a life of sobriety
and sanity and happiness. So is she.
So are your kids. Never forget that.

♦ ♦ ♦

*W*hen children start getting in trouble,
make the hard decisions together.

Problems

$\mathcal{K}$eep in mind your children will
constantly watch both of you—
are you drinking, is she drinking,
are you taking pain pills all day?
What are you teaching them?

*U*nderstand problems will happen.
Problems are part of life . . .
divorce doesn't have to be.

*R*emember you made an oath
before God to love her forever, not just
to love her during the good times.

Problems

Spend at least an hour talking with her
every night. This will eliminate a lot
of problems before they start.

● ● ●

The earlier you bring God into your marriage,
the stronger it will be.

*R*emember laughter and love
exit a marriage about the same time.

● ● ●

*R*ecognize something's haywire if you
regularly start losing your temper,
trying to change her, or trying to control
everything in her life.

Problems

*N*ever consider divorce as an option,
and it won't be.

*D*on't be her enabler if she's drinking
or using.

$\mathcal{R}$ealize grown adults don't get drunk or stoned. If you're doing one or both, then it's time to grow up.

♦ ♦ ♦

$\mathcal{D}$on't expect perfection out of her or you. Life will be smoother.

*R*emember these statistics:
25 percent of marriages have to deal
with alcoholism, 22 percent with drug addiction,
28 percent with infidelity, 40 percent with
a financial crisis, 100 percent with each other.

$\mathcal{D}$on't get mad because she gets afraid.
Understanding, love, sympathy, and talking
go a long way during tough times.

● ● ●

$\mathcal{B}$e able to talk about your problems
with other men. You'll be amazed how many
have walked in your shoes.

Problems

*B*e willing to do some things without her that further your own spiritual growth. This could be dinner with other men, going to ball games, or going to a prayer group.

♦ ♦ ♦

*R*ealize no situation is hopeless. And as long as you're together, you can survive anything.

*R*emember, an affair doesn't just happen.
It's a decision, one that you can decide
not to do.

*E*xpect a miracle every morning.

Problems

$\mathcal{T}$urn your marriage over to God, praying that His will be done. This will mean, of course, that what you want will no longer matter.

• • •

$\mathcal{I}$f she says or does something to upset you, think before you react.

$\mathcal{R}$ealize any addiction is a sickness—
just like cancer or heart disease.

$\mathcal{D}$on't go to bars or clubs without your wife.
You'll get what you deserve,
and she deserves better.

Problems

Remember, there isn't a marriage problem
that love, compassion, forgiveness,
and kindness can't solve.

And you may be the *one* who has
to offer them first.

$\mathcal{D}$on't make her guess if something's wrong.
It's astonishing how many grown men
act like small children when it comes to
communication with their wives.

♦ ♦ ♦

$\mathcal{I}$f you find yourself even thinking about
having an affair, act like an adult and
seek professional and spiritual guidance.

Problems

From day one, make sure she believes you'll stand by her.

• • •

Don't be afraid to join a support group if you have to. It will help both you and her.

Realize you both have your own paths to follow,
you both have your own problems to solve,
and until you heal individually, you'll never
heal as a couple.

• • •

If a marriage counselor hasn't made a
difference in six months, go to another counselor.

Problems

$\mathcal{D}$ecide to *love* her . . .
no matter what.

You have that power.

*I*f you can't let her live her life
without criticism or control on your part,
you have a problem.

*C*risis in a family is inevitable.
Letting a crisis rip your marriage apart is optional.

Problems

$\mathcal{E}$arly on, develop a relationship with your
priest, rabbi, or minister. They will be a
touchstone to the spiritual for you.

♦ ♦ ♦

$\mathcal{F}$orget the ridiculous idea that one
of you can "go home" to the parents.
You are home. Work it out.

Health

*T*ake care of yourself. One of your primary
jobs as a husband is to stay around.

● ● ●

*M*ake sure she gets regularly
scheduled checkups.

Health

Go with her to her mammograms.
It's incredible how many husbands will let
their wives go alone to an exam that could
change their lives forever.

*E*xercise. A fat, out-of-shape husband is as attractive as a fat, out-of-shape wife.

♦ ♦ ♦

*B*uy her sunscreen.

♦ ♦ ♦

*B*uy her a health-club membership.

*W*hen you get sick, she'll want to take
care of you. Let her for a while.

*U*nless you graduated from
medical school, realize most women
instinctively know more about taking care
of their children than most men. Biological fact.

Sex

*I*nvite God into the bedroom.

• • •

*S*how her affection throughout the day,
not just in bed.

• • •

*B*uy a book if you need to.

Sex

Shave.

♦ ♦ ♦

Remember the very worst thing
you can do to your sex life is criticize her
or make her feel bad about herself.

♦ ♦ ♦

Recognize that sometimes all she wants
is to be hugged.

THE
Husband Book

*R*emember the Cosmo girl is fiction.

*N*ever use unsatisfactory sex as an excuse to fool around. She's probably having as bad a time as you are.

Sex

If a two-year-old has been throwing up on her and she's been sitting in a car pool lane with the air conditioner off and she rushed to put dinner on and her mother is giving her grief, realize this might be a bad time.

She really might have a headache.

● ● ●

Learn how to give her a massage.

● ● ●

Have a good travel agent.

S_{ex}

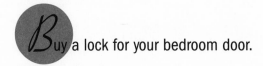

*B*uy a lock for your bedroom door.

*R*emember that nothing
temporarily ruins sex like a baby.
For both of you.

$\mathcal{D}$on't be afraid to talk about sex with her.
Most men find this as difficult
as speaking Latin.

♦ ♦ ♦

$\mathcal{S}$tart early. Even the most passionate parents
find themselves unconscious by 10:30 P.M.

Sex

Don't believe what you read
in the magazines.

Introduce your kids to
Saturday morning cartoons.

*C*ontinue to make *passes* at her.

Even when she's seventy.

$\mathcal{C}$ome home regularly with flowers.
You never know when it will pay off.

● ● ●

$\mathcal{R}$emember, criticism is not an aphrodisiac.

● ● ●

$\mathcal{I}$f you are a kind and considerate lover,
don't worry about your "performance."

"How would you like to go to Hawaii?"

Chores

$\mathcal{D}$on't think there are women's chores
and men's chores. You could wind up
sleeping on the couch.

♦ ♦ ♦

$\mathcal{D}$on't think that you can go play golf while
she cleans the house and does the cooking.
Another couch causer.

Chores

*D*on't confuse obsessions with chores. If you're obsessed with having an award-winning yard, don't expect her to share your enthusiasm or concern.

*I*f you think laundry is a woman's job, you've lost contact with reality.

*T*each your children to be *useful* around the house and the yard.

This will pay off years later.

*R*ealize that a man's natural inclination around the house is to put things off, while a woman's is to strike before the sun's up.

*T*each your kids to take care of their chores before they go have fun. It will save your wife's sanity and help prepare your kids for the real world.

*L*earn when to call an expert.
Don't install a garbage disposal just because
your neighbor has a nifty new blowtorch.
You'll still have to call a repairman . . .
only now it's going to be real expensive.

● ● ●

*D*on't assume that because she's a she,
she knows how to sew.

Chores

*P*lant flowers for her. Do everything within your power to ensure they won't die.

♦ ♦ ♦

*N*ever let her feel that all the housework is up to her.

♦ ♦ ♦

*F*old the laundry. Half of it's yours anyway.

Vacations

$\mathcal{D}$on't make the mistake of believing that
just being with you is a vacation.

• • •

$\mathcal{F}$ly first-class when it's just the two of you,
even when you can't afford it.

• • •

$\mathcal{R}$ealize she needs a vacation
as much as you do.

Vacations

*I*f you have kids, buy the biggest mode of transportation you can afford, ideally with bucket seats in back so nobody has to touch.

*D*on't complain about money the whole trip. In fact, figure out how much you can spend, then make it a point to spend every penny.

*D*on't go crazy when things inevitably go wrong. Your reaction will dictate whether the family can relax and laugh about it or be miserable.

*W*hen traveling with the kids, get them their own room.

Vacations

$\mathcal{I}$f you're driving, get a *map*.

And for *once* in your life,
be willing to ask directions.

*R*esolve to take one family vacation a year.
Not one a decade.

◆ ◆ ◆

*Y*ou'll want to get there in a hurry. She'll want
to enjoy the drive. It's up to you to compromise.

◆ ◆ ◆

*G*et away with her alone at least once a year.
Even if only for a weekend.

Vacations

Remember, a trip with just her is a vacation.

A vacation with her and the kids is a trip.

Maybe a fun trip. But a trip.

● ● ●

Time-share condos are great deals,

if the housework is also shared.

As the kids get older, they'll
want to *do* things. By themselves. Like ski.
Or golf. Or snorkel. Or go to the clubs.

Which is not *all* bad news.

*S*he doesn't want to

go to Disney World

with you.

She wants *Maui*.

(See "Sex.")

Stay in a suite with her.

♦ ♦ ♦

Order room service for her.

♦ ♦ ♦

Some weekend, take her
to a bed-and-breakfast inn in the country.
Even if you miss a football game.

Vacations

$\mathcal{T}$ake her shopping in
$\mathcal{N}$ew $\mathcal{Y}$ork, $\mathcal{S}$an $\mathcal{F}$rancisco,
$\mathcal{L}$os $\mathcal{A}$ngeles, or *overseas*.

(See "Sex.")

*O*nce in your life, book a surprise vacation,
just for the two of you.

*E*ven if you've lost your job,
don't cancel your vacation plans with her.
Find a way to go.

Vacations

Menopause

*R*emind yourself that millions of men have successfully lived through this experience.

● ● ●

*D*on't count on a lot of sleep after three A.M. until all this passes.

Be *flexible*. She will be hot.
She will be cold. She will be suicidal.
She will be ecstatic.

And this will all be within a
thirty-second period of time.

*R*emember these words:

"*It's my fault.*"

Regardless of the facts.

*R*ealize that during this time, photos will make her cry, school plays will make her cry, Toyota commercials will make her cry, and it won't help to try to explain how the commercial was just a fairy tale.

*D*on't be surprised when she talks about how warm she is, even though the temperature is hovering around 1.

*R*emember, this is a time when women tend to watch *Oprah* a lot. And cry.

Menopause

$\mathcal{B}$e ready to apologize instantly for the slightest infraction, like asking, "How do you feel?"

♦ ♦ ♦

$\mathcal{T}$alk about what you'd like to do
when the kids have graduated, after you've retired.
Stay on the same wavelength.

*A*pproach her birthdays with caution.
She may not want to mention them or,
even worse, she may demand to be taken
to Hawaii for treatment.

♦ ♦ ♦

*D*on't expect her to be any happier
on your birthdays.

Menopause

Tell her how great she looks
in reading glasses.

• • •

If she's in a fighting mood, leave.

• • •

Never comment on how wet
her side of the bed is in the morning.

*E*ncourage her to take her hormones.

● ● ●

*G*et her to a doctor. For her sake.
And yours.

● ● ●

*N*ever, ever dismiss something she says with
"It's just your hormone imbalance."

Menopause

*B*ecome deaf to criticism.
It's the best way.

Anniversaries

$\mathcal{T}$hank God for every one of them.

$\mathcal{R}$eally celebrate the big ones.
This will usually involve jewelry or a trip.
Or both.

Anniversaries

*M*ost of the time, flowers will do fine.
Even cheap flowers.

♦ ♦ ♦

*F*ailing flowers, a book of poems you would
never read will do in a pinch.

*B*uy the mushiest, most sentimental card
you can. If she cries, you've scored.

(See "Sex.")

$\mathcal{D}$on't even think
of giving her two tickets to the game
as an anniversary present.

Home and
Home Repair

*I*t doesn't really matter
if you're king of the castle.

It's *her* castle.

Don't try to impress her by installing the dishwasher. Hire a plumber.

If she's convinced the house has to be remodeled next week, go get a loan.

*I*nvariably, she'll want to hang pictures whenever there's a tied game with two minutes to go. Turn up the volume.

*G*et her to believe that when you've changed a light bulb you've accomplished something significant.

Home and Home Repair

Smile and nod whenever you find yourself
in a furniture store. Even if you're nodding
at a ten-thousand-dollar bed.
Smile and nod.

*N*o matter how easy it looks,
don't wallpaper a room yourself.

• • •

*Y*ou may not think the room needs painting.
Smile and nod.

You may not like the color Harvest Peach.

Smile and nod.

*S*he will never understand your
primal need for a wall-sized, high-definition TV
with a quadraphonic surround-sound system.
Help her with this.

♦ ♦ ♦

*R*ealize, of course,
she may never let you turn it on.

Incredibly, she will prefer
a washer-dryer combo over a big screen.
You'll *never* figure this one out.

● ● ●

*B*uy her a computer of her own.

Entertainment

*R*emember these words:

"*I think I've watched enough football today. What would you like to do?*"

$\mathcal{T}$ry doing different things at night: chess, Monopoly, even reading. After you have kids, sleep will be a highly prized form of entertainment.

◆ ◆ ◆

$\mathcal{J}$ust because you grew up playing hockey doesn't mean she shares your passion.

*D*on't be jealous when she beats you
at card games.

*T*ake her out on a picnic.
For some reason, women love them.

Entertainment

$\mathcal{B}$e willing to break the routine
every now and then.

$\mathcal{D}$on't think she's interested in
only hundred-dollar dinners.
Most wives are content with a simple meal
and just being with you.

*I*nvest in a *hot tub*.

(See "Sex.")

$\mathcal{D}$on't be afraid of thinking of things to do
she might shoot down. It's part of the
communication process.
And she will surprise you often.

● ● ●

$\mathcal{L}$earn to really and truly love antique hunting.

$\mathcal{D}$o not think for even one minute that she will ever enjoy a monster-truck pull.

• • •

$\mathcal{R}$emember that a marriage is made up of two *individuals* . . . one who might like hockey on Friday night with his friends and another one who might like movies on Saturday with hers.

"Yes, I think this painting will look great in our living room."

*R*emember, doubles tennis is *never* recommended to strengthen a marriage.

♦ ♦ ♦

*W*hen you play together, hold your criticism.

♦ ♦ ♦

*S*he doesn't really care about winning. She just wants to have fun and be with you. This is a foreign concept to most men.

$\mathcal{D}$on't use golf as a reason to be gone five hours a day, three days a week.

• • •

$\mathcal{I}$nvest in a croquet set.

• • •

$\mathcal{B}$uy her a bicycle. Buy yourself one too.

Music and the Arts

$\mathcal{T}$ake her to a flower show once or twice a year. Smile and nod at the other husbands.

♦ ♦ ♦

$\mathcal{D}$ance with her in the kitchen.

♦ ♦ ♦

$\mathcal{B}$uy a piano.

$\mathcal{T}$ake her to the symphony, to musicals.

You might like them. $\mathcal{Really}.$

*I*f your children are practicing their tuba lessons, confirm her thoughts that they could be really big stars.

*T*ell her often she has a great voice. Even if there's evidence to the contrary.

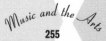

Music and the Arts

*W*hen she wants to drag the whole family to a museum thirty miles away, tell the kids it's important they understand the Impressionist period. Let it go at that.

*D*on't think because you were once in a band, she's dying to hear you play. She's lying.

• • •

*C*onvince her a concert would be worth the hassle.

• • •

*L*earn to love art galleries.

*S*he'll insist the kids learn to play piano.
Smile and nod. That will take care of itself.

♦ ♦ ♦

*G*ive up the idea of the velvet Elvis painting.

♦ ♦ ♦

*B*uy her a stereo that fits on a shelf. Listen to
her music at breakfast and dinnertime.

*J*ust because she went with you to
seedy country-and-western bars
fifteen years ago doesn't mean
she liked it then.

Or *now*.

*W*hen she mentions vacationing
in Amsterdam so the two of you can study
the Dutch Masters,

smile and nod.

Money and Finances

*S*pend below your means.

● ● ●

*R*emember the most important thing
you can offer her besides love is security.

● ● ●

*B*e home for dinner. Even if you have to drive
back to the office after you eat.

*I*f she's home raising children, remember it is as exhausting, frustrating, and exasperating as your job. Only with no retirement plan.

♦ ♦ ♦

*B*uy an insurance policy.
Make sure she can live on the proceeds.

♦ ♦ ♦

*A*gree on your dreams.

*A*ccept the fact that you'll never feel
like you've made enough.

*R*ealize her natural instinct is to "make"
the home. And this requires things
that cost money.

Don't ever succumb to the belief
that if she gets this one more thing—like a
new couch—she won't want anything
for another year.

If you want to know where the money goes,
go grocery shopping sometime.

*I*nvest in checkbook software, such as Quicken. It's a marriage saver because it tells you where all the money's going . . . which might surprise you.

• • •

*R*ealize some of your stupidest fights will be over money, so try to avoid them.

$\mathcal{B}$oth of you should have some allotted mad money that you can do anything with, without worrying what the other one will say.

♦ ♦ ♦

$\mathcal{I}$f you think her expensive obsession with her clothes is odd, just how weird is it smoking ten-dollar cigars?

Get a financial counselor
that both of you respect.

♦ ♦ ♦

Don't blame her for spending everything.
If she's doing the food shopping, buying the
children's clothes, and paying the bills, it's a
real possibility that she *is* spending everything.

*P*ray to God for wisdom about money.

*R*emember that God has a plan for you,
and even though it may differ from your plan,
it will fill you with wonder and awe
if you talk to Him about it regularly.

*S*ome women make more than their husbands. Instead of feeling guilty, enjoy it.

*D*on't think you have to tell her everything that's on your mind.

*I*f the stock market crashes,
come home with flowers.

*M*ake sure she has credit cards,
checkbooks, and money. At all times.

*B*efore you question her spending,
take a long look at yours.

• • •

*S*tart a retirement plan. Today.
It will make her feel better.

*S*eek her council on the family attorney, the stockbroker, the banker.

*S*he'll honestly tell you that you work too hard. She'll be secretly grateful too.

*N*o matter what, don't let yourself feel like a bad provider.

That's *just* the kind of thing that ends marriages.

*L*et her manage the checkbook.

◆ ◆ ◆

*I*f money is tight, pay the bills together.
It's less scary.

◆ ◆ ◆

*G*ive her an IRA of her own. Every year.

*I*f you can't talk to your wife about money and sex, your marriage has zero chance of making it.

*S*he'll do without a lot of things so her kids can have everything. It's up to you to bring some balance here.

*S*he'll drive across town to save $1.50.
Enjoy the ride.

● ● ●

*O*nce or twice a year, take her on an
expensive shopping trip.

● ● ●

*S*eek her guidance about all things financial.
You're in this as a team.

*R*emember, businesses come and go.
Investments go south. The smartest bankers
routinely make bad decisions. Money problems
don't have to be the end of the world . . .
or a marriage.

*N*o matter how hard you try, there will be some times when you just don't make enough. Don't feel guilty.

♦ ♦ ♦

*E*ven when money is tight, figure out a way to give back to God. This is a spiritual requirement.

She doesn't want as big a house as you think.
Or might want yourself.

♦ ♦ ♦

She'll spend all the money on the kids,
then tell you that you have to make
more money because she doesn't have *any*.
Smile and nod.

Money Troubles

The fear that you will lose your job will keep her awake at night.

You will *never* understand why.

$\mathcal{I}$f you do lose your job, don't retreat from her.
Tell her what's going on with you, and what
you are doing about it.

$\mathcal{F}$ailing cash to solve a problem,
have a plan B.

$\mathcal{D}$on't let her feel she has to figure it all out.
Because she thinks she does.

● ● ●

$\mathcal{I}$t doesn't matter if you have lived well
for twenty years, you're going to feel like the
worst provider in the world during these times.
Limit your self-pity. Get moving.

She's going to fall apart the first time the kids have to do without. Logic and history won't help here. Solutions will.

While you don't want to think about money problems, she wants to talk about them at 2:30 A.M. Avoid a fight. Talk about it.

*A*gree with her on a time every week when you can go over all the bills, the debts, and the prospects. Stick to it.

♦ ♦ ♦

*R*ealize there will still be back-to-school clothes, soccer dues, and electricity bills. Just saying no isn't going to work. Make a plan.

Money Troubles

$\mathcal{D}$uring this time, don't beat yourself up about putting everything on a credit card.

• • •

$\mathcal{S}$he may blame you for everything at these times. Forgive her.

• • •

$\mathcal{R}$emind her, you can go through anything together.

$\mathcal{G}$et on your knees and give this problem
to God every morning. This is as much
a spiritual issue as it is a fiscal issue.

$\mathcal{D}$on't lie around the house.
Get up every morning, go for interviews,
network, attack the problem.

Money Troubles

*R*ealize when she gets the most scared is
when she feels the most powerless.

◆ ◆ ◆

*W*hen this is all over, do not hold
her anger or her words or her fear against her.

◆ ◆ ◆

*R*ead Psalm 91 together every night.
It will sink in after a while.

*I*f you have a once-in-a-lifetime event planned and suddenly you lose your job, don't cancel your plans. Go.

Even if you have to *charge* the whole thing. Go.

$\mathcal{T}$his is absolutely not
the time to start drinking.

● ● ●

$\mathcal{A}$ccept the fact that sometimes God
wants us to do something different, so if we
can't take a hint, he just gets our attention.

*A*gree to go for a drive if she needs to cry or yell.

● ● ●

*D*on't keep your children in the dark. They can tell something's wrong.

● ● ●

*D*on't be embarrassed to downsize. She'll be more for it than you think.

Money Troubles

$\mathcal{D}$on't lose your inner joy.

♦ ♦ ♦

$\mathcal{T}$rust that God will take care of you and her.
Let her know this is at the core of your being.

♦ ♦ ♦

$\mathcal{D}$on't count on money from her parents.
Or yours.

*I*f you have to sell your Rolex to make
the mortgage payment, sell the Rolex.

♦ ♦ ♦

*I*f she's depressed during these times,
don't let her stay in misery.
Do what you can to lighten the mood.

Money Troubles

When it's all over, she'll tell you
that she never lost faith.

Smile and nod.

Intimacy

$\mathcal{D}$on't make her feel like every time you kiss
her you want to have sex, as hard as that may be.

● ● ●

$\mathcal{I}$nstead of getting up first thing
in the morning, hold her for a while.
You'll come to treasure those moments.

Intimacy

*I*gnore her bad habits.

*H*old her hand all the time. In the movies.
Walking. Watching TV.

*C*onsciously smile at her.

Even when you're exhausted. The payoff is big.

♦ ♦ ♦

*I*f she has a dream about you
having an affair, she will wake furious.
No amount of logic will help here.
Just hold her.

Intimacy

$\mathcal{D}$raw her a bubble bath. Then leave.

● ● ●

$\mathcal{T}$reasure those times when you can just sit
and read and enjoy each other's company.

● ● ●

$\mathcal{R}$emember, there are few aphrodisiacs
more powerful than just listening.

Food and Meals

"This tastes great."

$\mathcal{R}$ealize no one wants to do the dishes . . .
especially the cook.

◆ ◆ ◆

$\mathcal{A}$ccept that while a man can live
on barbecue alone, most women can't.

*E*at at places other than steak restaurants.

*M*eet her for lunch someplace
if she can get away—this brings about
all kinds of wonderful things.

(See "Sex.")

*D*ress for dinner. Some men think
they can show up in their boxer shorts
and their presence alone will carry the day.

• • •

*I*f you're going to be late for dinner, call her.
You're never too busy to be considerate.

*G*o to the grocery store for her. You can bring home stuff she'd never buy.

*W*ake up early every morning and cook her breakfast. You can pretty much get away with murder the rest of the day.

She won't believe beer
is one of the basic food groups.

♦ ♦ ♦

If she wants to make the family dinner
every night, count yourself very lucky.
And show up on time.

*U*nless invited, do not under
any circumstances venture into the kitchen
to adjust the heat, add ingredients,
or check the taste.

◆ ◆ ◆

*T*he reason you don't know why
you need a Dutch oven is because
you don't know what it does.

Food and Meals

When you or the kids get sick, something genetic inside her will make her cook soup. With noodles.

Enjoy it.

$\mathcal{W}$hen she makes a meal that is
truly horrible, you have two choices:
shut up and make dinner the next time or
shut up and eat it. If it's that bad,
she'll notice too.

$\mathcal{R}$emember ketchup and steak sauce
can hide the taste of just about anything.

Food and Meals

*W*hen you are really hungry for a steak,
and you come face-to-face with an artichoke,
and she's real happy with everything . . .

smile and nod.

• • •

*N*o man has yet figured out what women like
about pimento cheese sandwiches.

*E*very now and then, take her to a truly fussy, lace-on-the-walls, high-tea-served place to eat lunch. Order the chicken.

*R*emember one of the great things about being married is that a woman can never finish her dinner. So you get more food.

Food and Meals

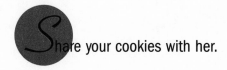 hare your cookies with her.

Let her have the last piece.

Pets

*I*f your dog seems to love her more,
it's because dogs aren't stupid.

♦ ♦ ♦

*I*f she can't watch her kids get a shot,
she won't be able to watch her pet get one either.

♦ ♦ ♦

*S*he may never enjoy your kid's hamsters.
Or snakes.

Pets

*I*f you find yourself spending more money
on the pet's food than your food,
it's time to have a talk.

● ● ●

*S*he will always side with the dog.

● ● ●

*T*he dog will figure this out.

*I*f you get two pets and one of them
is hers and one of them is yours,
guess which pet sleeps in the bedroom.

P_{ets}

Her Car

*D*on't let her drive the oldest car in
the garage. Either you drive it or get a new one.

♦ ♦ ♦

*L*et her pick out her own car.
Help only if asked.

♦ ♦ ♦

*R*eset her car clock as daylight saving time
comes and goes.

Her Car

*I*f you have small kids, it will be better for everyone if you never look in her back seat.

● ● ●

*C*heck the air in her tires.

● ● ●

*M*ake sure she gets her oil changed every three thousand miles.

$\mathcal{D}$rive her car every three or four months
to see if, for some unexplained reason,
the wheels need to be aligned.
Quietly take care of it.

$\mathcal{T}$he garage wall will every now and then
reach out and hit her car. It's the garage's fault,
of course.

Her Car

*S*he will put the most expensive gas
in her car, required or not.

*B*ehind every woman in a clean car
is a man with a chamois.

You may love your '84 diesel Mercedes, but she'd rather *walk* than drive it.

Her Car

Your Work

$\mathcal{D}$on't make work your life. Some of the most successful businessmen are some of the most unhappily married men.

● ● ●

$\mathcal{Y}$ou don't have to go to bars after work with the boys. Go home.

Your Work

$\mathcal{Y}$ou don't have to carry the pressures
of your work all by yourself. Talk to her.
Let her know what's going on.

$\mathcal{D}$on't regard your work as some
inner sanctum where you can't take care
of family business.

*I*nvite her to your office.

♦ ♦ ♦

*R*emember, she loves you fiercely.
If she perceives you're being taken advantage
of at work, she'll be looking in the
yellow pages for a hit man.

Your Work

*I*f she's a stay-at-home mom,
never throw it in her face that you have a job
and she doesn't. She has a job.

She just *doesn't* get paid.

*M*ake sure she can reach you at any time.

♦ ♦ ♦

*C*arry your cell phone. Answer her calls.

♦ ♦ ♦

*I*f you come home from the office mad,
remember who you're mad at. And it's not her.

Your Work

*E*ven if you have to work on Saturdays, you can still have breakfast with her.

● ● ●

*B*e sure your priorities are in order:
God, family, work.

*I*f she's not a risk taker, starting your own company may scare her to death. There's nothing you can do—ten years later, when you're very successful, she'll still be afraid.

*I*n fact, she may think of "self-employment" as another word for "unemployed."

Your Work

Stability is extremely important to her.
If you go six months without making money,
then suddenly make $100,000,
she'll just remember the six months
without money.

♦ ♦ ♦

Hire her to keep your company's books.

*M*ake sure she understands this isn't your company but the family's business. She'll be more accepting of business cycles if she feels some ownership.

◆ ◆ ◆

*I*f you work together, take some time to mess around and have fun.

Your Work

*E*njoy the fruits of your success.

With her.

Her Work

*D*on't be afraid or jealous of her success.

● ● ●

*M*arvel at her capabilities.

● ● ●

*B*e her fan.

Her Work

*R*ealize what she most wants from you
is support.

*S*end flowers to her office.

When she rants and raves about work,
just listen to her. She doesn't want your help;
she wants you to listen.

Don't leave all the housework to her.
She's as tired as you are.

Her Work

Celebrate her achievements.

♦ ♦ ♦

Let her know that what she's doing
is important to you.

♦ ♦ ♦

Don't compare salaries.

$\mathcal{F}$ill her car up with gas Sunday night.

♦ ♦ ♦

$\mathcal{E}$ncourage her to get massages.

♦ ♦ ♦

$\mathcal{H}$ave her boss over for dinner.
Be on your best behavior.

Her Work

She will meet a lot of people who will become very important to her. Don't trivialize these relationships.

● ● ●

Make sure she has an umbrella.

● ● ●

If she's not happy in her work, encourage her to try something else.

The Best Years

*B*uy a smaller home. She'll want cozy.
You'll love the payments.

*D*o all the things you couldn't do while there
was soccer practice, weekend tournaments,
proms, and homework. Like sleep in on Saturdays.

The Best Years

You'll be amazed how you can love this woman more today than you did twenty-five years ago.

Buy two La-Z-Boys.

*T*ake her shopping at all the places
you couldn't afford when you had
college-tuition payments.

♦ ♦ ♦

*M*ake sure your kids understand
when and where your monetary support will end.
By now, she won't fight you on this.

The Best Years

$\mathcal{W}$hen the kids come home in the summer, she will act as if they're ten years old and need constant mothering again. If they didn't like it, they wouldn't come home.

$\mathcal{A}$dopt an older dog. Already house-trained.

$\mathcal{E}$njoy the routine.

● ● ●

$\mathcal{Y}$ou'll notice some nights it's you
who has the headache. She won't care.

● ● ●

$\mathcal{T}$ake long walks in the park.

The Best Years

*T*alk about where you really want to live.

*W*hen she says she always wants
the kids to feel like they have a room of their own,

smile and nod.

$\mathcal{M}$ake sure she takes her calcium pills.

◆ ◆ ◆

$\mathcal{G}$o to the mountains in the summer.

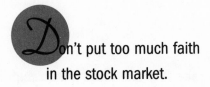

*D*on't put too much faith
in the stock market.

*T*hank God for your marriage every night.

Every Morning

*S*tart a new affair with her.

Every Morning